The Quitter's Manifesto

THE QUITTER'S MANIFESTO

Quit a Job You Hate for the Work You Love

TIM RHODE AND PAT HIBAN

**BiggerPockets®
PUBLISHING**
Denver, Colorado

The Quitter's Manifesto: Quit a Job You Hate for the Work You Love
Tim Rhode and Pat Hiban

Published by BiggerPockets Publishing LLC, Denver, CO
Copyright © 2022 by Tim Rhode and Pat Hiban
All rights reserved.

Publisher's Cataloging-in-Publication Data
Names: Rhode, Tim, author. | Hiban, Pat, author.
Title: The quitter's manifesto : quit a job you hate for the work you love / By Tim Rhode and Pat Hiban.
Description: Denver, CO: BiggerPockets Publishing, 2022.
Identifiers: LCCN: 2021950317 | ISBN: 9781947200678 (hardcover) | 9781947200685 (ebook)
Subjects: LCSH Vocational guidance. | Job satisfaction. | Self-employed. | Business enterprises. | Entrepreneurship. | BISAC BUSINESS & ECONOMICS / Careers / General | BUSINESS & ECONOMICS / Entrepreneurship | BUSINESS & ECONOMICS / Motivational | SELF-HELP / Self-Management / Time Management | SELF-HELP / Personal Growth / Happiness
Classification: LCC HF5381 .R46 2022 | DDC 650.1--dc23

Published and printed in the United States of America
10 9 8 7 6 5 4 3 2 1

DEDICATION

Pat dedicates this book to Tim, for being the first person he ever met who lived a life of interest instead of obligation.

Tim dedicates this book to Pat, who followed in his footsteps and came up with the idea to write this book.

TABLE OF CONTENTS

PART III: *SWING!*

INTRODUCTION
Everybody Loves a Quitter

It's been said that an entrepreneur is the kind of person who jumps off a cliff and builds an airplane on the way down. For some people, this is exciting stuff. They're the "leapers," and the idea of flinging themselves off a cliff is exhilarating. Whether it's changing jobs or starting a business, they happily plummet toward the ground, building wings and whistling a cheerful tune. *Any minute now,* they think, *I'll have this plane finished. What a ride!*

Good for them. But not everyone is a leaper. For most of us, leaping is terrifying. When it comes to big life changes, we'd rather take the stairs one at a time, thank you very much.

That's why quitting is hard. Leaving a secure job, the steady paycheck, and the benefits? Quitting is like leaping—it's tough. And if we *have* to jump? Most of us aren't enjoying the scenery and constructing wings—we're screaming in terror and watching our lives flash before our eyes. Instead of building an airplane, we're frozen. *This was a terrible, terrible idea,* we think. *What's going to happen? What if it doesn't work out?*

Here's a secret: There are a lot more non-leapers than leapers in the world. A *lot* more. Most people are intimidated by big changes, and few changes are bigger than upending your stable job for something new.

You might be a non-leaper. After all, if you were a leaper, you'd have leapt already. And you probably wouldn't be reading this book. But if you've been thinking about quitting for months or even years, you're not alone.

Let us help you feel even better. The critical thing most people don't talk about is that leapers fail a lot. To be clear, some failure is good—that's how you learn. But leapers are like the BASE jumpers of quitting. They crash frequently and the consequences are painful. Sometimes they don't build those airplanes in time. Or when they do build them, they don't work like they're supposed to and things get scary.

Not only is it okay to be a non-leaper, but it may also be an advantage. If you want a professional change but aren't keen on dashing out of your current job like the place is on fire, then this book is for you.

TAKE A LOOK AT THESE QUITTERS

We're Pat and Tim, your hosts for this journey, and we're Quitters. Pat left a thriving real estate career—like, a seriously thriving one. And sometimes it feels like Tim has quit more things than he's started, if that's even possible.

By almost every measure, we've been extraordinarily successful. We have great relationships. We're healthy. We're financially secure. We've built exciting, abundant lives that fit our values and make us feel like our time here on this planet really means something. In other words, quitting has served us well.

You're going to hear more of our stories in the pages ahead, as well as the stories of other Quitters who found their way from something they didn't want—and in some cases never wanted—to something they really did. People who were unhappy, unfulfilled, or unrewarded, and quit to find better lives.

Some went from full-time jobs to starting businesses. Some went in the other direction. Some became freelancers so they could finally be in control of their professional lives. Others switched from one job to another.

You'll hear from them, in their own words, in the pages ahead—people like you, who became successful Quitters. People like:

- Sean, who worked in sales and now operates his dream business—with a dream income too.
- Jessica, who grew increasingly disillusioned as a teacher and quit to start her own school.
- Debbie, who quit a high-paying management position so she could be there for her kids when they needed her most.
- Gabriel, who left a minimum-wage job to find joy and financial freedom in real estate.
- Jake, who realized after losing his father that he could fulfill both their dreams by starting his own business.

- Carole, who went from a full-time job to "retired" with her own small business, a new home, and time for her next adventure.
- Joseph, who quit a draining six-figure job to buy three businesses.

In each case, they approached that intimidating cliff of change in their own way. And in each case, they succeeded—no BASE jumping required.

These are wildly different people leading very different lives. But along the way, each person discovered the same thing: quitting isn't simply the entry point to new work; it's a portal to a whole new world.

TWO TRUTHS ABOUT QUITTING

This is as much a book about changing your mind as it is about changing your work. Yes, changing your work is the endgame. But getting there is trickier than people realize, largely for two reasons.

1. Quitting is an inside job.

It feels like an *outside* job. It feels like it's about taking action. You have to write the resignation letter. Possibly tell your boss to shove it and storm out in a whirlwind of dramatic *humph*. And there's the other stuff. Like finding new work or starting a business, networking, and dusting off the resume. That's all "action stuff" that takes place outside of you.

To be clear, most of the action stuff is necessary. (Although you might choose to forego giving your boss a piece of your mind or throwing your desk out the third-floor window.) But if the action stuff was all that was stopping you from finding the right work, you probably would have leapt off the cliff long ago—or at least rappelled down in a secure harness. And you certainly wouldn't be reading this book.

Quitting is about action, yes. But it's far more about why you *aren't* taking action.

So, why aren't you? That's part of the road ahead: dealing with the inside job. The uncertainty. The programming. The fear. The it's-always-been-this-way-so-I'll-just-keep-doing-it trick that your brain keeps playing on you.

That's the real job at hand. And it's why you'll find that this book isn't prescriptive. We're not going to tell you exactly what steps to take to get job X or start business Y. How could we? Even if we could, it wouldn't be helpful because—to really hammer the point home—*that's not the problem*.

2. Quitting is often slower and more subtle than you think.

Sometimes people change in an instant. They call it an "epiphany." It happens in the movies all the time. One minute our hero has a job she hates, and a scene later she's ditched it all and has a trendy SoHo loft.

In our experience, epiphanies are rare. People don't usually change in an instant, especially on the inside. Most often, change is far more gradual, and the inside job of quitting often takes time.

In the pages ahead, you'll learn how to think differently about change, and you'll feel more hopeful that you can actually make change. Because you can.

ONE YEAR FROM NOW

It's said that nobody loves a Quitter. What this really means is that we aren't inspired by someone who gives up—not on the task at hand, but on *themselves*. Consider that your new job: to not give up on yourself. Don't quit your quit.

When you feel stuck, remember that somewhere out there is someone very similar to you. They have bills to pay and obligations to meet. They have a mortgage or rent. Student loans. A couple of kids. And they are doing the very thing you want to do. All because they never gave up on themselves. They didn't quit their quit.

Isn't that inspiring? Someone out there has found a way to get past every obstacle you face. Which means it's possible. You just have to start. A year from now, you'll wish you had started today. So, start today. Right here. Right now.

Pat Hiban and Tim Rhode

PART I
THE CLIFF

*Why Quitting Is So Hard
(And What to Do About It)*

WELCOME TO THE CLIFF

Imagine you're standing at the edge of a cliff. Looking out, you can see something beautiful on the other side of the enormous chasm in front of you. The gentle breeze feels nice, but it's a sheer drop, and just peeking over the edge is enough to make you a little queasy. You retreat.

The land on this side of the cliff is "now." It's safe. It's where your comfy routine is. Your steady job with the benefits and the familiar commute and the predictable paycheck. (That paycheck is never as big as you'd like, but it shows up like clockwork.)

Over on the other side of the cliff is what you want. What is that, exactly? If you already know the answer, good for you. If you don't, that's fine, because the more pressing question is: Why are you still here? If the other side is where you want to be, then why haven't you left already?

The answer is probably that big, scary cliff. The cliff is what makes change hard. Change isn't a real cliff, of course; it's a metaphorical one. You aren't going to die if you quit your job.

But the feeling is similar. Where you are is safe, but taking that first step feels like an impossible leap.

That sheer drop—that big scary cliff—has been keeping you stuck in place.

How do you unstick yourself?

ACKNOWLEDGE THE TRUTH

Your first job while staring over the edge of that cliff is to realize that quitting your job isn't really about quitting.

Sure, it's easy to make it about that. You can dig into how much you earn here versus there. You can compare benefits and talk about health plans. You can even talk about the lifestyle benefits of this job versus that one, or the value of finally being your own boss.

But quitting isn't a pros and cons list. Leaving the predictable job that supports you and that has become part of your identity is hard because it's *uncertain*.

Cliffs are uncertain. They make you feel like you might fall.

Quitting is uncertain too. It makes you feel like you might *fail*.

Your brain hates uncertainty. You've been wired through a zillion years of cave-person ancestors to be a prediction machine. It's how you made it this far. And now you want to jump ship? You want to leave the predictable hours, the known coworkers, and the reliable paycheck for some unpredictable thing? Forget about it. Your brain hates that. Too many unknowns.

For your brain, uncertainty equals risk.

For your brain, the danger of falling and failing is the same thing.

It's all one big, scary cliff.

In evolutionary terms, when you see a cliff, you step back. When you fall off a cliff, you don't get to have babies and have your DNA live on. To be absolutely certain that you get the message, you've evolved the perfect tool: fear. Faced with uncertainty, you get scared. It's as simple as that. It's nothing to be ashamed of because it's your greatest survival tool.

But it also keeps you stuck. The uncertainty makes you nervous. The nerves make you start thinking, *What if? What if I lose my life savings? What if I fail? What if I can't support my family? What if I don't like the new thing? What if I'm embarrassed?*

All that what-if-ing raises the stakes even higher. It's the emotional version of standing on the edge of a cliff and thinking, *What if I fall?* The fear generated by that uncertainty is enough to keep you from straying too close to the edge. It lowers your risk and keeps you alive.

These days, you don't face many literal cliffs. Things are pretty safe. But what about figurative cliffs? You're not thinking, *What if I fall?* But you are thinking, *What if I **fail**?*

Fall. Fail. For your brain, it's all the same.

TIME TO FACE THE SCARY MUSIC

The first tool in your toolbox, then, is to simply accept that change is hard and scary. That may seem simple, but it's harder and more complex than it seems.

Accepting the truth that some part of you is afraid of the

change isn't just about honesty. When you accept that fear is a factor, then you can stop making it about other things. You can accept that the reason you haven't changed yet isn't because of your benefits package or your mortgage. Those are important, but the real reason is that change is hard. It's hard for everyone. We're all human, after all.

Instead of a pros and cons list, make a list of all the reasons you can think of why you haven't already quit. Next to each reason, list what you think you're actually scared of.

Be brutally honest with yourself. Get real. It's where the good stuff starts.

TOOL #2

UNDERSTAND RISK AND REWARD

Change is daunting. Cliffs are scary. What are you going to do about it?

Leaping still is an option. Just *quit*. Jump. You can be like the entrepreneurs who build planes. Or the ancient warriors who burned their ships so they had no option but to succeed in battle.

Leaping has one remarkable advantage: It creates incredible urgency and focus. When you jump off a cliff, there's no question of where you're headed and how much time you have. You either start building wings or you crash and burn.

The abrupt quit is like that. It leaves you with little choice. You hand in your resignation and then you figure it out. It definitely solves the first challenge because it eliminates the pain of the job you're in. But it's also scary as hell, and it carries a higher chance of failure.

At the opposite end of the risk spectrum is the bridge. It's the safe way to get somewhere. It's when someone shows up and offers you your dream job out of the blue, or you get a chance to start a business that can't fail—with no money down and no hard work.

When you're facing the cliff, a bridge can feel like a handy thing. It's a safe, guaranteed way to the other side. It's not scary. You can't fall or fail.

But there are two problems. First, bridges are rare. Albino-tiger rare. It's unlikely that someone will arrive out of the blue and offer you your perfect job or business. That's like being plucked from a crowd at the mall to become the next famous actor. It can happen, but it's not something you want to bet your future on.

Second, bridges are actually *too* easy. Too safe. That guaranteed safe delivery comes with a price: Bridges tend to lead you to similarly safe places. In the real world, the biggest, safest bridges are built from one popular place to another. They're crowded.

When you take that similar job with the similar benefits that showed up in your inbox from some recruiter, and it feels safe and easy, you're probably headed somewhere you've already been. You're probably trading a job that doesn't fulfill you for one that will eventually leave you feeling the same way.

YOUR MOST IMPORTANT CONNECTION

In investing, there's a relationship between risk and return. When you invest in something safe—bonds, for example—you get a lower return. Invest in something riskier, like stocks, and your returns tend to be higher.

But just because you invest in something riskier doesn't mean you get more returns automatically. Risk just creates the *possibility* of returns. Taking risk opens the door to something better.

The same is true of work and life. Risk and reward are con-nected. If you play it safe and don't try anything new, deviate from your routine, or leave the good job you hate, you tend to get lower returns in life. You have less opportunity, less pros-perity, and less joy. You meet fewer people and feel less alive.

Add a little risk, however, and life delivers a whole new kind of richness. No risk, no reward. You don't have to get crazy. You don't have to leap. But you have to take *some* risk. If you're waiting for a no-risk reward, you're going to be waiting a long time.

QUITTERS LIKE YOU

SEAN ADE
Owner, Roosevelt's Terrariums

I've never been a great W-2 employee.

As a twenty-year-old, I knew I wanted to be my own boss. I just didn't know how to get there. At twenty-three, in my first years as an inside-sales rep, I ranked No. 1 in a $2 trillion company and was immediately moved to outside sales.

I reached my ceiling pretty quickly and then there was no way for me to grow further within the company. At first, I thought I'd hold onto the job and buy real estate. But after getting my Realtor license and juggling a W-2, being a Realtor just wasn't for me, and so I held onto my W-2 job.

For years I wanted to quit, but that steady paycheck and easy work-life balance made it so hard. I just kept hanging on. I always told myself an excuse for why I couldn't quit.

Then 2020 happened. I was furloughed and the world turned upside down.

I was talking with a friend who was adamant that this was the time to buy small businesses. I had never thought of buying a small business before, only of starting one, but I decided this was my move.

And that is what I focused on every day for four months. Every day I told myself I was going to buy a business, but I didn't know what type. At first, I looked at what everyone else looked at: laundromats, car washes, landscaping, plumbing. But none of these was right because none of them interested me.

Then in the middle of July, as I was taking care of my plants, it struck me that I needed to own a plant store. My home is covered in houseplants. I just love them. They make my place look better, they calm me down, it's fun to repot them and propagate them. I love plants.

I went back to my journal and wrote, *I'm going to buy a plant store in Portland that is closing because of COVID and has a baby boomer as an owner.* I'd gotten crystal clear on what I wanted and it was exciting.

I looked at a few businesses over the next few months, but nothing was penciling out. I would send possibilities to a knowledgeable friend for consideration. Within thirty seconds, he'd reply, "No way. Find something else."

I started to get a little discouraged, and then another idea hit me. Why not reach out to my network? I was fairly active in a few Facebook groups about trading plants. (Gotta love Portland.) I typed up a thoughtful post about how I was looking to help small-business owners that are closing due to COVID, and asked that if anyone knew of one to please connect me with the owner.

Within hours, someone posted that Roosevelt's Terrariums had announced they were closing. The owner was sixty-eight years old, with no debt on the business, and was closing because of COVID. Exactly what I had written down!

I immediately called the owner and said, "Hey, my name is Sean. I heard you were closing. I wanted to see if you'd rather sell me your store."

He loved the idea and sent me his financials. He also said he needed me to buy within two weeks.

After reviewing the numbers with my friend, he negotiated the price down, with 100 percent owner financing. I ended up paying $5,000.

The store had never sold anything online. Everything was brick-and-mortar. I opened up shipping, e-commerce, and virtual events, and the momentum started building. Within three months of owning the store, I paid myself my first owner's draw of $24,000. It was the best, smartest, and boldest decision I've ever made.

THE LESSONS

Get clear about what you want.

Tell everyone.

Be bold; risk and reward are conjoined twins.

ASK THE FAILURE QUESTIONS

If the world's greatest motivational speaker showed up at your house tomorrow morning, they might try to inspire you with "the question."

You know the one: "What would you do if you knew you couldn't fail?"

It's not a bad question. In fact, you might want to answer it right now. You might find some insight there.

But that question breaks the rules of risk. It asks you what you want with no risk. In reality, you already know what you get by taking no risk: more of whatever situation you already have.

Perhaps it's time to add a follow-up to the famous failure question: What if you're *already* failing?

If you run a business that goes bankrupt, it's painful, but you call it a failure and move on. If your relationship fails, it's painful, but you move on.

Is what's happening right now a failure? Is your safe, unfulfilling situation a failure in and of itself? If so, it's time to get real and acknowledge that. It's time to declare a new kind of bankruptcy and move on.

Let's push our failure question set even further. What would you do if you knew you *would* fail?

Author Seth Godin asks this question in *The Practice*. It's a question designed to open your heart and mind to the thing that's worth doing even if it fails. That thing might not make money. But it might bring you riches in other forms. It might bring you clarity. It might save you from future regret, which is perhaps the highest form of success there is.

Go ahead and ask yourself the failure questions.

ASK THE FAILURE QUESTIONS

What would I do if I knew I couldn't fail?

_____

_____

_____

Am I already failing in my current job?

_____

_____

_____

What would I do if I knew I *would* fail?

_____

_____

_____

TOOL #4

ACCEPT THE REALISTIC WORST-CASE SCENARIO

Andrew desperately wanted to quit his accounting job and start his own business. But every time he thought about making a change, his mind went into full-blown catastrophe mode. He imagined how his business would fail, and how then he'd lose his home and his wife would leave him and take the kids. Soon, he theorized, he'd be sleeping in his car. Then, he'd have to sell the car for food and he'd be homeless. After a few years of hard life on the street, he'd likely die of an infection.

This was the exact scenario that went through Andrew's mind. Starting a business meant he was going to *die*. It wasn't true, of course. But for Andrew's brain, it felt true, and that was enough to keep him stuck.

With some help, what Andrew eventually did was accept the *realistic* worst-case scenario. Death, he realized, wasn't a realistic worst-case scenario if he were to leave his accounting job. Andrew had great relationships at his firm. So great, in fact, that he could leave on good terms to start a business—and get his old job back if it didn't work out!

The realization was a game changer. Now the worst-case scenario was a measurable financial one. Andrew determined how much he'd have to invest in his new business and how much time he'd need to get it going. Losing that money—the forfeited salary, plus his startup costs—was the realistic worst-case scenario.

Next, he asked himself if he could accept this new worst-case scenario. He also talked it over with his wife. The answer was a resounding yes, and he never looked back (or died).

MAKING PEACE WITH PLAN B

The worst-case scenario isn't the worst thing that could possibly happen. It's the worst *reasonable* thing that could happen connected to what you're trying to accomplish.

The worst-case scenario tool is about making peace with Plan B. It's there so that when things get uncertain (which they will) and you feel uneasy (which you will), you can remind yourself that you've already accepted that you can live with an unsuccessful outcome, should it occur. This will prevent your risk-predicting, fearful ancient brain from catastrophizing—then you can get on with your new life.

FOLLOW THE FEAR

Here's what we've learned so far:

1. Quitting is about dealing with fear.
2. Fear is there because there's some risk involved, and your brain doesn't like that.
3. Risk, however, is connected to reward. There's no risk-free plan that will get you what you want.
4. Getting clear about that risk and accepting the realistic worst-case scenario can help you get past that hurdle.

There will be times ahead, particularly when you start to take action toward what you really want, when things will be hard. You will feel nervous. You will be scared. Not only is this okay, it's also perfectly normal. Remember, fear is what got you and all your ancestors this far. If you didn't have it, you'd be (a) not human and (b) not here.

Embrace the fear. Call it what it is. But don't let it pilot the plane. Because although your brain might think that falling and failing are the same, *they are not*. One kills you. The other sets you free. Because fear can set you free, that means you need to follow it.

Don't worry, you don't need to throw yourself off the cliff. Right now, all you need to do is burn this into your brain:

Fear of quitting isn't a sign of danger.
It's a signpost pointing the way.

In those moments when you feel uncertainty, your nerves get jangly, and the idea of change makes an anxious hollow in your stomach, know that your body is pointing at something important. Don't look away.

PART I CONCLUSION

A NOTE FROM TIM

By my late thirties, I felt like my career in sales had oxidated. I'd wake up each day feeling like my use-by date had passed. I was becoming old and sour before my time. I desperately wanted change. I had no idea what was next, but I knew my professional life no longer served me.

The problem was The Committee. The Committee made it almost impossible for me to change. Every time I'd start to even think about something new, The Committee would shut it down almost immediately. I felt like I had no control over my future.

It was a difficult time in my life. And it was made even more difficult by the fact that The Committee *was all in my head*.

The Committee had two main leaders. One was the mean, belittling Dickhead Boss (DHB) who would bark at me to prospect for new clients daily. The second leader was the Scared Kid who hated rejection and feared the DHB.

Each day, the DHB prodded the Scared Kid to get on the phones, screaming, "YOU SUCK. YOU HAVEN'T DONE SQUAT. GET ON THE PHONES NOW." Each day, the Scared

Kid in me would cower, feel ashamed, and wish for the courage to make a change.

Eventually, the Scared Kid did stand up to the DHB. But the first step was to realize that change is an inside job. There was really nothing in the outside world stopping me. The only obstacles were on the inside.

It's very tempting to believe that things on the outside—things like paychecks, nest eggs, benefits, and salaries—are the obstacles to moving forward. But those risks are usually small compared to the emotional risks. Things like the fear of failure. The fear of what others might think. The fear of being judged or dismissed. The fear of The Committee in your head.

You can try to avoid those fears by not taking emotional risks, but that's where the sweet stuff is. It's where you have to go. You move toward the discomfort of the new thing. You move toward the bees for the sweetness of the hive.

ASK YOUR FUTURE SELF

Time passes. There's no way around it. Every year you make a trip around the sun, and just like that, you're a year older.

A helpful way to start bolstering your courage to quit is to think of the Future You—you know, the one who's going to be standing where you are after that next trip around the sun.

What will Future You really wish you'd done this year?

Sometimes, that question can feel a little difficult to dig into. Here's another way to look at it. What, at this moment, do you really wish Past You had done last year?

If Past You had quit last year, how would you feel right now? What if Past You had started the side hustle? Opened that business? Written a few pages a day? What if you'd reached out to that person you met? What if you'd taken the improv class? Learned to code? What if Past You had decided that the risk was worth it?

No matter what, a year is going to pass. Your journey around the sun will continue. The only thing you can control is what you choose to do with the time.

MORE PIE

There's an old joke in legal circles that making partner at your law firm is like winning a pie-eating contest where first prize is more pie. There's some truth to this joke. Lawyers are notorious for working themselves to the bone to make partner, only to have to work even longer hours once they finally "arrive."

The lesson for you, the prospective Quitter, is to beware of getting more of what you already have. The cliff may be scary. Quitting the safe thing may feel daunting. But the reward you get without risk is more pie. More of the same. More of what you're sick of. Full of. Can't stand.

Rewards are almost always on the other side of something that's harder than we would like. Change begins with digesting that truth. Change, however, doesn't happen just by peering over the edge of the cliff and saying, "Yep. That's scary." Quitting, in the end, is an action.

In Part II of this book, we'll teach you how to build your own Quit Plan using two approaches: the trapeze and the net.

KEY INSIGHTS

TOOL #1

ACKNOWLEDGE THE TRUTH

Quitting is scary. For your brain, it's like standing at the edge of a steep cliff. That fear is the real thing keeping you stuck.

TOOL #2

UNDERSTAND RISK AND REWARD

Risk and reward are connected.
There's no risk-free quit.

TOOL #3

ASK THE FAILURE QUESTIONS

What would you do if you knew you couldn't fail?

What if you're already failing?

What would you do if you knew you would fail?

TOOL #4

ACCEPT THE REALISTIC WORST-CASE SCENARIO

The realistic worst-case scenario is far less scary
than you think. Can you accept it?

TOOL #5

FOLLOW THE FEAR

Fear is a sign of something important.
Sometimes, you need to follow it.

QUITTERS LIKE YOU

JESSICA SERRANO
Cofounder, Ignite Academy Inc.

The bell had just rung at end of a particularly long school day, and I had retreated to my office in the back of my fifth-grade classroom. Surrounded by piles of ungraded papers and teaching curriculum, I looked up at the bulletin board hanging on the wall. Between pictures of former classes and sweet notes from students, I eyed an old, slightly worn copy of one of my college papers. While in my master's program, we had been asked to write our philosophy of education, and here it hung five years later. I took it off the bulletin board and sat down to read what I'd written before I ever led a classroom.

Flipping through its pages, I remembered the excitement and optimism I'd felt as I had considered the boundless potential of every child, the learning strategies that would help them unleash their growth, and my personal thoughts on what education should be. I was a teacher in my twenties now and still equally passionate about education. However, after a few years in public school, I had begun to develop a deep sense of longing. A tension began to arise as I considered what I believed to be true about learning, growth, and development. I loved my coworkers, my school, this mission, and more than anything, I loved my students. I was really good at my job. But was I doing what was best for these kids? Was the system I was part of aligned with my values as a teacher? Staring at that college paper was like looking into a mirror where my reflection was incongruent with the person I wanted to be.

Change isn't always instantaneous. It starts with small feelings of misalignment and evolves into a cavern of dissonance that you can no longer ignore. There are hints along the way, whispers that remind you of what could be and what you could do. During this same school year, I became pregnant with my first child, and maternity leave from my teaching position loomed in the distance. I knew a break was ahead, and maybe, just maybe, this change of pace would allow me to pursue these thoughts further and see where what-if could take me. While in my birthing center's waiting room, I picked up a magazine and came across a full-page graphic with a quote that would forever change my life. The background featured a decaying stump with a small sprout of vibrant green growing from its center. The quote read, *You never change things by fighting the existing reality. To change something, build a new model that makes the existing model obsolete.*

I had been trying to transform an entire educational model from within the walls of my classroom. I had been fighting against the strong current of county requirements and government reforms. Although I had made a positive impact on the few families and students I was blessed to serve, what about the hundreds of other children who were not getting what they needed from our current educational model?

So, I quit. I turned in my resignation letter, and I quit a perfectly good job. It turns out that sometimes, saying no to something is really just saying yes to something better. I did not know what that would look like, but I was confident that God would do much with this simple act of faith. I committed the next few years of my life to walking down uncharted paths. I said yes to experiences in different educational environments, including homeschool, private school, and curriculum development. I said yes to helping my husband learn how to lead a business. I said yes to building relationships with parents and discovering what they wanted in a school, and I said yes to dreaming even more about what education could and should be.

Three years ago, I cofounded a nonprofit called Ignite Academy Inc. and we launched our first elementary school in Palm Harbor, Florida. The school started with seven families, and now we have a waiting list and plans for future locations. It's a school that aligns with my values as a mother and educator. It's an idea that came to fruition because I had the audacity to quit, to pivot, and to bravely venture into what could be.

THE LESSONS

Change happens slowly, and then all at once.

Have faith.

Saying no to something is a way of saying yes to something better.

PART II

THE TRAPEZE
AND THE NET

*How to Quit
without Leaping*

THE TRAPEZE AND THE NET

It's clear now that what you want is on the other side of a deep chasm of uncertainty. Figuratively speaking, you're standing on a high cliff staring into the distance at a new job or a new business, but the scary, unknown space in between is holding you back.

You also know this:

There's no zero-risk plan that will get you to the other side.

To get to what you want, you have to face the unknown. You have to take risks. But how much risk should you take to get what you want? So far, your options are unattractive:

- Leaping is high-risk. It's painful, it's hard, and if leaping were your jam, you'd already have done it.
- Bridges are low-risk. Too low, in fact. They take you to places you've already been.

This conundrum is keeping you stuck. You never quit—you just keep talking about quitting. You keep wishing and dreaming and what-if-ing. It's all ready, aim, ready, aim, ready, aim.

You're not alone. Every Quitter faces this same dilemma and the only way out is to *act*. Right now, however, you're stuck.

Here is the real challenge facing Quitters everywhere:

How do you make change when change is hard?

Enter the trapeze and the net. When a circus performer wants to get from one high place to another, they use a trapeze. It's too far to jump, so they swing from one trapeze to the other, like a nimble monkey swinging from vine to vine. Each trapeze is a safe spot on the journey across—like baby steps for high places.

Sometimes, of course, trapeze artists fall. It happens. You can't avoid every mistake. That's what the net is for. It's a safe place to land when stuff happens. The trapeze and the net are your solutions to being stuck because they help you feel safe enough to take the first steps across the chasm of uncertainty.

The tools that follow will help you set up your first trapeze moves or help build your safety net—or both.

Ready?

TOOL #6

CHECK THE SUCK METER

There's an old story about a fertilizer salesman who shows up at a farmhouse to sell his wares.

The farmer's dog is sleeping on the porch next to him, and as the salesman does his pitch, the dog keeps lifting his head to whimper and moan.

The salesman asks, "Is your dog sick?"

"Nope," says the farmer. "He's just lyin' on a nail."

"Well, why doesn't he move?"

"It ain't hurtin' him enough yet."

If you've been standing on this side of the chasm for years, this could be the dilemma you're facing. It's not that you aren't excited about the prospect of a new job or starting your own thing. But the pain of staying put is like the nail—it ain't hurtin' you enough yet. As long as the pain of staying put is tolerable, you'll never grab that first trapeze bar, no matter how close it is.

JUST HOW BAD IS IT?

Tim's approach to this challenge is to use what he calls the "suck meter." It's a strategy for making the pain of staying put more tangible—for making that nail hurt more so you can take your first trapeze swings.

There are two parts to the suck meter.

1. The present. How much does your current gig suck?
First, let's get real about exactly how bad things are right now. Rate the following on a scale of one to ten, and average your five scores:

- Your compensation
- Your respect
- Your fit for the team and organization
- Your prospects for growth
- How you feel each morning about facing the day

Every job or career has some measure of soul-suckage. Nothing is perfect, and every type of work has its good and bad. But if you can't clear a six on average, then, as Tim would say, the soul-suckage is far too high.

2. The future. How much will regret suck?
Sometimes, just putting a number on things and saying "This is how bad it is" can help to get you unstuck. Often, however, you *know* how high the suck factor is each day, but it still isn't enough to make you reach for that first trapeze bar.

Let's look to the future, then, to try to assess the cost of what hasn't happened yet. Ask yourself these questions:

- If I never quit, how will I feel when I'm seventy years old?
- What will it be like to never achieve the income I've always felt I could?

- What will I be like as a person if I keep doing this for another decade?
- How will I feel about explaining to my kids why I stayed in a job I hate?

These things are harder to put numbers on, but they're important because they represent a different kind of pain. They clarify the soul-suckage that your future self will experience if you never take that first step. This pain represents the cost of *not* quitting, and it stacks up under one big suck category called "regret."

Regret is nasty business. Regret pushes the suck meter into the red zone. The problem is that you don't feel regret until it's too late. It's the pain of a road not taken and now lost forever, and it only comes in hindsight.

SHARPEN THE NAIL

Author Tony Robbins writes, "Change happens when the pain of staying the same is greater than the pain of change."

In other words, change doesn't happen when where you're headed looks good enough. Change happens when where you're standing *sucks* enough. If you've been lying on a nail that just isn't hurting you enough, then perhaps it's time to sharpen it. Get clear about the true cost of doing nothing. It just might help you reach for that first trapeze bar.

WEAVE YOUR FINANCIAL NET

Money lurks in the back of every Quitter's mind. A financial net might not be the only net you need, but it's almost certainly going to be the one that preoccupies you the most.

Nets are similar to those planes that entrepreneurs create— trying to build one after you've lost your grip on the trapeze bar is stressful and has a higher chance of failure. The smartest time to build a net is before you need it. Here's how:

1. Get real.

You cannot build a financial net with your eyes closed. You have to get honest and real about *exactly* where you stand. This isn't always easy, but it almost always makes you feel better after you do it. When it comes to money, the truth helps.

To get real about your financial situation means two things. First, you must determine how big your net is. This is the stuff on the "good" side of the money equation, like:

- Current income from all sources.
- Savings.
- Other assets—investments, real estate, crypto, etc.
- Access to credit.

Second, you must determine the size of the holes in your net. The holes in your net are things like:

- Your "burn rate"—your monthly bills/cost of living.
- Debts, including loans, leases, mortgages, and credit cards.
- Other financial obligations—payments to retirement plans, investments, health care, etc.

This is no time to hide from unpaid bills or to be unsure just how much is left on that student loan or car lease. A net with holes can still save you, but you have to know where those holes are.

2. Get credit now.

Part of your safety net can be access to credit that you can use if things get dicey or take longer than they should. Your credit net can include:

- Credit cards.
- Account overdrafts.
- Home equity lines of credit (HELOC) or other credit lines.
- Private loans/other options.

If you wait until you really need credit, you're going to have a tougher time getting it. The time to get that HELOC is before you're struggling to make your mortgage payments.

Now is also a good time to renegotiate terms where you can. For some debt, this is as simple as just asking!

3. Build an emergency fund.

Everyone needs one of these—not just Quitters. You can start building an emergency fund that works with your budget in two very quick steps.

- **First, open a separate, free savings account at your bank.** Make sure—and this is important—that you do *not* attach it to your bank card or your phone where you have easy access to it. If you can tap, swipe, or click to pay with this account, you did this step wrong. Do it again.

- **Second, set up an automatic, regular transfer from your main account to this new one.** How much? That depends on your income and burn rate. If you think you can do 10 percent of your income, go for it. If you think you can't, then pick a lower number. We suggest you *double* your first instinct—you can almost always save more than you think. Make sure it's *automatic*. If it's not automatic, then you did this step wrong. Do it again.

That's it. Two steps.

If you've done this right, then a small amount of money will be transferred automatically on a regular set date into your new "hidden" account, where it can stack up without you spending it or having to decide whether or not you can afford to save this month. The process matters more than the amount. Just get started.

GOOD NETS MAKE FOR GOOD THINKING

In their book, *Scarcity*, authors Eldar Shafir and Sendhil Mullainathan showed that not having enough money has such a profound impact on an individual's psychology that it can actually inhibit the brain's functioning. Financial scarcity consumes more of our cognitive bandwidth and gives us a kind of tunnel vision, making it harder to think and act in ways that serve us best in the long run.

In other words, feeling like you don't have enough money makes you dumber.

Note that this is about the *feeling* of not having enough. Remember how we said quitting was an inside job? It matters less what your financial situation is going into your quit and more how you feel about the situation.

Your financial net isn't just about having some extra cash for when stuff happens. It's also about giving you the mental space to make the best decisions possible about your future.

QUITTERS LIKE YOU

DEBBIE BOMAN
Massage Therapist and Real Estate Investor

About ten years ago, I was in a management-level career with Marriott at their spa in Las Vegas. I was very proud of my job. I was putting in sixty hours a week, but I was making great money. I was a single mom, but I could afford the things my kids were into, like tennis. I was feeling really good about myself.

But a lot happened when my kids were teenagers. They were missing both their parents, and they needed me. I was working so many hours and was away from home a lot. It really caused me to reflect. Knowing something had to change, I left my management job to work on my own as a massage therapist so that I could be more available for my kids.

I started exploring ways to market myself, and through much research, I gained some hard-won insights from books like *Think and Grow Rich* and *The Miracle Morning*.

For the next few years, as I worked for myself, I was able to pay my bills. I was doing okay. But I had even bigger career aspirations, and so I decided that when my kids graduated from high school and were ready to become more independent, I would go into real estate.

When the time came, I sold my house in Vegas, moved to the Oregon coast, and bought my first short-term rental property. It's doing extremely well. I'm in the process of buying my second one—it's attached to some commercial property, so it will be mixed-use, which I'm super excited about.

For the first time in my life, I'm really feeling the momentum in my career, and I feel like I'm where I should be. I know that's because I did my research when I started my journey so that I would know what I needed to do, and so that I'd feel confident about doing it.

My advice to single moms or anyone who is trying to figure out how to work for themselves is to invest in your education, and put what you learn into action. Don't just read the books or listen to the podcasts, but follow the advice you are given. There are many people who have done this already. Do what they tell you to do and it will be life-changing.

THE LESSONS

Investing in yourself builds confidence.

When you find good advice, take it.

Follow the paths of those who have done what you want to do.

DECIDE WHAT SUCCESS LOOKS LIKE

Remember that old proverb about climbing the ladder of success only to find it's leaning against the wrong wall? That applies to more than just career-building—it's true of anything you chase in life. If you're going to start climbing something new, now is the time to ask yourself a few key questions.

1. How will I know if it's working?

This may seem simple, but it's worth it to clarify your metrics so you can gauge how it's going. What do you think making progress in your new job or business looks like? Progress could be:

- Feeling fulfilled in your new thing.
- Hitting certain metrics in a business, like sales, client, or profit numbers.
- Feeling more aligned with what matters to you, whether that's the flexibility to be home with kids, more vacation time, greater upward mobility, or something else.

This is essentially about defining the rungs on the ladder—or the next platforms to swing your trapeze to, if you will. What are the waypoints that will let you know you're getting somewhere? Where is your trapeze swinging *to*? How will you know if you're swinging in the right direction?

2. What success would I be happy with?

Remember that time you got the shiny new car, or the latest phone, or those fancy shoes? Pretty exciting … for a little while. Then the newness wore off, and the car just got you to work, the phone just let you communicate, and the shoes kept your feet dry.

This adaptation to things is called the "hedonic treadmill," but it's also called just plain "being human." We all struggle with it, but you can take the step right now of defining what you think would make you happy in the future. Then, when you reach those inevitable moments where you want *more*, you can say to yourself, *Hey. Remember when you said you'd be thrilled if you could ever earn X from this business?*

This is about defining a potential top of the *current* ladder. There's no rule that says you can't start climbing another one, but it's good to remind yourself of your original goal so that you can (a) celebrate it when you get there and (b) stop moving the goal post to your own detriment.

3. What would be an indication that I should quit?

We don't subscribe to the "never give up" motto. This is, after all, a book about quitting. Instead, we're into *strategic* giving up. Sometimes, things don't work. Other times, things work, but they don't work as you planned—they don't give you what you wanted, or they're not what you want anymore.

How will you know if you should quit your quit? Here are a few options:

- **Time commitment.** If your new business isn't working out after X months or years, is it time to consider quitting?
- **Financial result.** If you aren't making X at a specific time in the future, is it time to bail?
- **Fulfillment level.** If the new thing sucks or isn't what you thought it would be, is it time to move on?

These questions are about avoiding the sunk-cost fallacy—our tendency to keep going because "we've already come this far/invested this much," etc.

DEFINE SUCCESS AND FAILURE BEFORE YOU QUIT

The magic in determining what success and failure look like *now* is that you capture your answers before they inevitably shift over time. By defining what you're leaning your ladder against, and how many rungs it takes to feel like you're making progress, you create something you can refer back to in the future.

If you hit an obstacle on the road ahead, you might feel an urge to quit. But if you've already decided what the terms of quitting are, then you can either say, "Enough," or "No. This isn't a full failure. This is a challenge. I shouldn't quit." Either way, you will have full confidence in your decision.

BUILD YOUR PLAN B

When a trapeze artist falls into a net, they're not just stuck there—the net stretches to absorb their fall and then bounces back so they can get to the edge and climb out.

Part of your net-building will help you bounce back when you fall. To do it, create options for possible Plan B scenarios if things don't go as expected. Here are three common categories for backup plans. A great quit will have at least one option in each.

1. Go back.

French essayist Joseph Joubert once said, "Never cut what you can untie." One Plan B option is to simply go back to how things were. You might go back to your old job (with a fresh perspective), or you might go back to similar work for a different company. In either case, as long as you haven't burned those bridges, you've got a great net in place.

2. Pivot.

This word has been embraced by the startup community to mean changing the strategy for a business venture, but it can apply to anything. If you've quit your job to start a landscaping business, a pivot might be to take your skills and interest to a related business, like property management, or in a different direction entirely. There's no rule that says you have to keep swinging in the same direction.

3. Get a side hustle.

The previous Plan B options fall into all-or-nothing categories. What about a middle ground? Let's say your new venture is doing just okay. Things are tight, but you're making progress. You're happy, you're getting somewhere, but you're also running out of runway. What do you do? One option is to pick up a part-time job or side hustle. Is it ideal? Perhaps not. Is it better than giving up or pivoting? Maybe.

PLAN B HELPS YOUR PLAN A

Creating a Plan B is close to Tool #4 (Accept the Realistic Worst-Case Scenario), but it's not the same. When you accept the realistic worst-case scenario, you're making peace with the possible downside. In this case, you're deciding what action you will take if that downside arrives.

Don't think of Plan B as a failure. Think of it as part of your safety net. It's like an emergency kit you keep in the trunk of your car—you don't want to use it, but having it on hand is just smart. Best of all, creating your Plan B actually helps with Plan A. Like a financial net, having a solid backup plan lets you think clearly and move forward knowing that you've got a safe place to go if things don't work out. That's what nets are for—letting you reach as far as possible with the knowledge that things will be okay if you slip.

GATHER YOUR QUIT TEAM

Quitting often feels like a solo act. It's *you* who has to quit. It's up to *you* to start the business or find the new job. But the game of quitting is best played as a team sport. Before you quit, we strongly advise you to build a Quit Team to support your transition. Here's why:

- **Your Quit Team builds your network.** Every person you involve in the process is someone who brings their own set of connections to the table.
- **Your Quit Team makes you smarter.** Many heads are better than one, and having more advice can be critical to avoiding pitfalls and making better decisions.
- **Your Quit Team keeps you grounded.** Quitting can be an emotional roller coaster. Having others around you helps you keep both your perspective and a level head.

Who's on your team? Generally, you'll find that the most important people you involve will fall into four categories:

1. Stakeholders.
These are the people close to you who have a real shared interest in your future. They're generally a spouse/partner, other

family members, and close friends. They care about you, and they also care about themselves. Your happiness and future are connected to theirs. These people have a real stake in your life; they're part of the team by default. Your job is to be transparent with them and ask for their support.

2. Partners.

These are people who provide critical ingredients that you can't get or help with things you can't accomplish alone. In business, they may be actual business partners, investors, key suppliers, or contractors. In your professional life, they might be key members of your network or existing customers, vendors, or suppliers who will play a pivotal role in your new career choice. Partners are excellent bridges to new opportunities

3. Mentor.

A mentor is someone who has already been where you want to go. In business, that's often someone who's built other successful businesses, especially in your industry. They help with strategy, experience, and advice that comes almost exclusively from the school of life.

4. Coach.

A mentor may bring professional wisdom and strategic guidance to the table, but a coach helps you create the mindset to do the necessary work, and holds you accountable to it. They'll also help you with any personal-growth areas you need to make your transition, and they will cheer you on when appropriate. Coaches aren't industry-specific. Choose a coach who can shore up your mindset challenges, not just your business or work ones.

YOUR QUIT TEAM IS A TRAPEZE AND A NET

Don't confuse these people with your network. They're part of your network, yes, but they're just a portion. Your Quit Team is a support system. It can be a remarkable combination of both trapeze (helping you find and take next steps) and net (helping you with slips and falls).

If you ever find yourself stalled or derailed in your quit process, that's the time to ask for Quit Team support. Do you need accountability (a coach)? Emotional support (a stakeholder)? Or do you need strategy, experience, and connections (partners and mentors)?

For each of the four categories, try to identify at least one possible team member. Start with a stakeholder—often a spouse or close family member. You'll need their support first and foremost.

Resist the urge to do this step later. You will learn an incredible amount from every person on your team, and the sooner you can connect to them, the more pitfalls you can avoid, and the more opportunities you will have.

You may find you don't have a person for every category. That's okay. Not every quit needs a big team. Not everyone needs a coach. But no quit should be entirely solitary. Everyone needs at least one close stakeholder, even if it's just for moral support and encouragement.

GATHER YOUR QUIT TEAM

Enter at least eight names into the categories below. Try for at least one name in each category.

1. STAKEHOLDERS

2. PARTNERS

3. MENTORS

4. COACHES

PLAN FOR OBSTACLES

Why? Because they're coming. There are difficulties, rejections, surprises, and setbacks in your future. There's no way around it.

Don't think of this as bad news. Remember, risk and reward are connected. If this were easy, everyone would already be doing it. Difficulties are part of the deal, but you'll feel better by preparing for them.

Of course, you don't know what those difficulties are yet, at least not all of them. You know gravity will try to pull you down when you reach for the next trapeze bar. But you can't anticipate the bit of grit that gets in your eye and makes you lose your grip. Gravity is the overall idea of risk; the grit in the eye is a specific event. You can assume the first, but you can't always predict the second.

To deal with this dilemma of planning for difficulties without knowing what they are, we do two things.

1. Envision what you can.

There are some challenges you can anticipate. If you're starting a wholesale import business, for example, you can anticipate shipping delays of goods that you ordered overseas. Those delays mean you've paid for goods but can't actually sell them yet. That means your cash flow is tight, and you might struggle to pay your bills.

This isn't a disaster. This is a problem you should *expect*. So, ask yourself, *What happens if my cash flow is tight?*

For example, you might think to yourself, *I prepared my financial net, so I know I have credit, savings, and access to a local business association that helps with small-business financing. If a hurricane slows down my shipment, then I'll use those tools to see me through.*

Your turn. Go ahead, ask yourself:

- What if it costs more than I thought?
- What if it takes longer than I thought?
- What if I'm only half-successful?

2. Plan your mental response to obstacles.

There are lots of things, like unexpected grit in your eye, for which you simply can't prepare. You can't see the future, and you can't plan for everything. But you can ask yourself how you'd like to think, feel, and behave when things get tough. For example:

- What kind of person do I want to be during challenging times?
- Who do I admire for their ability during difficult moments?
- How would I advise a friend or family member to stay mentally strong when things are hard?

Planning for obstacles won't help you avoid them; it will help you respond to them. Note that we say "respond" and not "react." That's the secret sauce of the net—the mental space to think more clearly when you face difficulty.

PART II CONCLUSION

A NOTE FROM PAT

I met my coauthor, Tim Rhode, at a seminar many years ago. I remember I asked him what he did for a living. He said, "I ski."

I ski? I wasn't even sure you were *allowed* to give that as an answer. Could that really be the answer to the question of what you do for a living?

Tim and I connected at that seminar and have remained that way to this very day. We're founding elders of the mastermind group GoBundance, and the two of us have been on so many adventures that I've lost count. In all our many years together, Tim has stuck with the same story: "I ski."

But here's the truth: Tim doesn't ski for a living. He's not a professional athlete, and he's not a ski bum. He engineered his escape from work as meticulously as anyone I know.

The best answer I can give to what Tim does for a living is that he evolves. He's a Quitter, but mostly he's a grower. He's like a snake that sheds its old skin because it's time to expand.

I quit real estate sales at the age of forty-six, and believe me, I had a hard time shedding that old skin. Quitting seemed to come naturally to Tim, but I struggled with it. Part of that difficulty was feeling like I wasn't leaving to grow. When the real estate market collapsed, the part of the work that I enjoyed most went with it. I liked making money. That was part of the juice I got from working. I liked being successful, I liked growing my business. I liked getting better all the time, and in my business, getting better meant earning more.

The mortgage crisis took that part away. It was like being at a great party when suddenly the music stops. Just like that, the energy was gone.

Rather than wait for the party to die completely, I decided I wanted to be in control. I wanted to choose my own exit. But that didn't make it easy.

In hindsight, what was so hard about my transition—and those of so many Quitters I've spoken to—is that quitting isn't just about changing your work. It's about changing your *identity*.

When you swing across the chasm between two cliffs, you're really transitioning to a new version of yourself. And that's not always easy. If you've always been a W-2 employee, then becoming an entrepreneur isn't just a job change. It's a shift in who you are. If there's one thing we like to hold tightly to, it's who we think we are. That's why the metaphor of the trapeze is so important. In order to cross the chasm, you have to be willing to let go of one trapeze in order to reach for another. It's a little scary and a little risky. But if you don't let go and reach, then you swing right back to being your old self in your old routine.

When we fail to make a change—like keeping a New Year's resolution, or creating a new habit, for example—this is part of what's happening. We're not letting go of the old identity to reach for the new one. We swing back, and the next thing we know, we've regained the weight, earned the same income, or failed to make some other change we so badly wanted.

Trapeze bars are really the baby steps of changing your identity. Just remember that the momentum that gets you started—that outbound, enthusiastic swing—can also carry you back to where you were if you don't learn to let go.

WHAT'S YOUR INTEREST/OBLIGATION (I/O) RATIO?

Entrepreneur and investor Naval Ravikant once asked a provocative question: "A personal metric: how much of the day is spent doing things out of obligation rather than out of interest?"

Like the suck meter, this question can help you let go of the trapeze by getting as clear as possible about the pain of where you are.

I've started asking this question on our GoBundance podcast, with a goal for members to try to live an 80:20 ratio—a life made up of 80 percent what interests you, and 20 percent obligation.

There are always obligations in life, and they matter. As much as we dream of a life with no obligations, it's not all that it's cracked up to be. But a life of all obligation is equally terrible. Why? Because an interesting life is also a happy life. If there's a secret to doing life right, that might just be it.

When your I/O quotient is high—when you get to do mostly what you're interested in—life is pretty good. But working a job that is soul-sucking, or that gives you no autonomy or sense of future, is by definition one of obligation. And that's a dead end every time.

Your trapeze might not take you where you expected. But every time you reach for something and decide to take the risk to swing into the unknown, just a little, it changes you.

And that change is almost always for the better.

KEY INSIGHTS

TOOL #6

CHECK THE SUCK METER

Change doesn't happen when where you're headed looks good enough; it happens when where you're standing sucks enough.

TOOL #7

WEAVE YOUR FINANCIAL NET

A financial net gives you the mental space to make the best possible decisions about your future.

TOOL #8

DECIDE WHAT SUCCESS LOOKS LIKE

Defining success now will help protect and motivate you in the future.

TOOL #9

BUILD YOUR PLAN B

A solid Plan B gives you the clarity
and courage for Plan A.

TOOL #10

GATHER A QUIT TEAM

Never quit alone.

TOOL #11

PLAN FOR OBSTACLES

Preparing for difficult times helps you respond
instead of react when they occur.

QUITTERS LIKE YOU

GABRIEL HAMEL
Real Estate Investor

I joined the Army National Guard during my senior year of high school. But when I graduated, I didn't know what I wanted to do next. I had only stayed in school for the social aspect and because I was a competitive wrestler. As a result, after graduation, I bounced between low-paying jobs and community college classes until I realized that college was *not* for me.

A couple of years after I finished high school, the book *Rich Dad Poor Dad* made it into my hands, and for the first time in my life, I read a book cover to cover, every last word. Before that moment, I didn't think I liked learning, but in reality, it was simply the first time I'd read about a subject that interested me. From that moment on, I decided that I would become financially independent and that the vehicle to do it would be cash-flowing real estate.

Shortly after deciding on my path to financial freedom, however, I was deployed to Iraq and Kuwait for over a year. I was often playfully ridiculed when I shared my dreams for financial freedom through real estate, but I was determined to come home after my deployment and get started on my plan.

After a year of looking, I purchased my first property with no money down, rented out two of the three rooms, and lived for less than I could have anywhere else. I purchased another home with no money down a year later and a third the next year with 5 percent down. Although these were subprime loans, I purchased well and made sure the properties would still be cash-flow positive when I moved out.

During those years, I had also opened up a small nutrition store, but the business just wasn't making any money. Meanwhile, my first son was born, and the bank guidelines had changed—they didn't want to lend me any more to purchase real estate. With more expenses and fewer loan opportunities, I shut the store down.

I was still nowhere close to my dream of financial freedom. I took odd jobs, searched the help-wanted ads on Craigslist, and pretty much took any other jobs I could find until eventually, I landed a minimum-wage job in a high school special education class. Three months into this job I found myself on my hands and knees, holding my breath, cleaning crap out of a bathroom stall that a student had thrown everywhere.

This was *not* my dream. I started thinking about the goals I'd set, and in that moment, I made a commitment to myself to get serious about going all in on real estate and replacing my minimum wage with rental income before the next school year started.

My job didn't pay much, so the goal felt very obtainable. I spent every night diligently searching Craigslist for seller-financed deals since bank loans weren't an option. I had many conversations with potential sellers and analyzed deals until eventually, I found "the one." It was a four-unit property that cash flowed almost to the dollar what I was making at my minimum-wage job. It was just $1,400 per month, so I wasn't wealthy yet, but I was financially free, and I didn't go back to work ever again!

I spent the next several years acquiring small multifamily properties. Each property was purchased using seller financing with no money down. My only requirement at the time was that the property be cash-flow positive.

Since those first three properties, I have never purchased another property using traditional financing. I currently own 226 units. That's 226 people who pay me rent, and I'm continuing to grow my portfolio in a way that allows me to focus my time and energy on my family, my health, giving back, and traveling.

THE LESSONS

You don't always need money to make money.

Sometimes you need to go all in to finally break free.

Don't quit on your quit!

Part III
SWING!

How to Keep Going When the Going Gets Tough

MOMENTUM TIME

It's said that 80 percent of success is showing up. There's some truth there. After all, you can't accomplish anything without showing up and doing what needs doing.

But that catchy little aphorism is also a bit misleading. It leads us to this kind of thinking:

- Want to be a bestselling author? Just publish a book.
- Want to run a successful business? Just rent an office.
- Want to be an influencer? Just create a viral video.

It doesn't work that way. You don't just show up once and succeed; you have to *keep* showing up. You have to keep writing, selling, filming, coding, cooking, or recruiting. In other words, you have to keep going.

When you watch a circus performer, the dangerous part of the trapeze that you *don't* see is the risk of staying still. The same is true of quitting. Cling too long to one bar, and you begin to lose momentum. Slowly but surely, the energy drains out of the system, and you end up just dangling. Stuck.

Eventually, you'll either fall from sheer exhaustion, or you'll have to go through the difficult process of "rebooting" your swing to get your trapeze moving again so you can reach for another bar.

Maintaining your momentum—letting go of one trapeze and reaching for the next—is what it means to show up. Reaching for that first trapeze bar is a courageous first step, but you can't stay there. You need to keep moving, trying, improving, and swinging. Do these things, and your chances of success keep improving along with you.

Once you start swinging, then, how do you *keep* swinging? Because you will be faced with reasons to stop. You'll find excuses to cling to the bar you're on. On many days, you may even find more reasons to stop than to keep going. Those are the days when you need to double down on your swing.

Welcome to the final set of tools in your Quitter's Toolbox. They'll teach you how to keep going when the going gets tough.

FAILURE-PROOF YOUR MIND DAILY

In the classic film *Lawrence of Arabia*, there's a scene where Lawrence lights a man's cigarette for him, then snuffs out the match using his bare fingers. When the man with the cigarette tries to copy Lawrence's move, he burns his fingers.

"It hurts!" he says, and demands to know what the trick is.

"The trick," Lawrence replies, "is not *minding* that it hurts."

Lawrence is clearly a never-give-up kind of dude. But he also has a thing or two to teach us about quitting.

Just as your quit will never be risk-free, it will also never be pain-free. There will be tough moments and hard days. This comes with the territory. The price of what you really want needs to be paid, and sometimes the price is doubt or pain.

But as T. E. Lawrence reveals, what successful Quitters are doing isn't a trick. It's not pain-free. They *do* experience doubt and worry. They *do* struggle. What they do differently is learn to tolerate it.

Professional athletes aren't superhuman; they get tired and sore. Professional Quitters aren't superhuman either. Like athletes—and Lawrence of Arabia—they learn to not mind as much. They understand that by learning to live with uncertainty, they're making a trade. They're accepting difficulty now in exchange for a much better future.

BUILDING A RESILIENT MIND

We call this "failure-proofing your mind." It's about preparing yourself mentally for the tough times that inevitably arrive, and, like building your physical muscles, it's a skill you can hone.

To be clear, we prefer our doses of pain and failure to be small. Lawrence of Arabia didn't snuff out a bonfire with his bare fingers, just a match. The best athletes endure *some* discomfort each day, but only enough to make them grow without injury. That's exactly how we want to treat your mind.

One Quitter had a great way to sum up the failure-proofing of your mind: "Each day, do whatever puts you in the best mental, emotional, and physical place to perform your best, stay positive, and be persistent."

How, exactly? When we look across all the Quitters we've known, there are common priorities and practices that make the difference. They include:

- Exercise.
- Journaling.
- Connecting with goals and progress.
- Meditation.
- Spirituality.
- Education.

Every successful Quitter we know has used at least some of these. It's how they stay focused and resilient during difficult times.

Note, however, that many of these things are solitary, and building resilience may require help from others. The tough times are when you need your Quit Team the most. This is the time for your partners, mentors, coaches, and stakeholders to shine. Don't hide the tough moments from them; their support may be exactly what you need most.

FIND THE SMALLEST POSSIBLE STEP

Every year, one-third of Americans do their taxes at the last minute. Come mid-April, they race against the clock in a frenzy of anxiety (and probably mistakes).

One-third of the United States is a huge number. It would be like the entire population of Japan or Mexico, all procrastinating at once. It's a lot of people.

You might be one of those procrastinators. If you are—or if you find yourself delaying other important tasks (like quitting your job)—allow us to give you the most important tool in the productivity toolbox. It works for small jobs like your taxes, it works for big, overwhelming projects, and it works for quitting your job. It's called the "smallest possible step."

Taxes are daunting. The forms are scary. Tax law is complicated. If you're like most people, the things you need in order to do your taxes are probably scattered about. Perhaps you have a shoebox of receipts. Or a file of digital forms. You might need to download statements from your retirement accounts. Oh, and there are those medical receipts ... Where did those go?

Taken as one, the job called "do your taxes" is a big, overwhelming, unpleasant to-do item. But what if you made it smaller? Like, as small as possible?

What if the first step to doing your taxes was *put the shoebox of receipts on the kitchen table?*

That's it. You put that item on your to-do list and nothing more. And you say to yourself, *This is the next step, and it's all I have to do.*

Because it's true. That *is* all you have to do. In fact, it's all you *can* do. You can only do one step at a time. You can't get the shoebox and sort the receipts and log in to your bank account all at the same time.

If you focus on that tiny step, and that step only, you'll find it's extremely difficult not to do it. In fact, you'll almost want to do it because it's clear, simple, and completely doable. It's an easy win.

Once you get that easy win, you might just decide to sort some of those receipts into piles.

SIZE MATTERS

Author E. L. Doctorow once said that writing a novel is like driving a car at night—you can see only as far as your headlights, but you can make the whole trip that way.

This is true of accomplishing all great things. You never really see the whole path laid out before you. You can't predict the highs and lows, the triumphs and failures. All you can see is the next part.

But it's *enough*. That little bit—the small next step—is enough to move you forward. And then you might just be able to see the next step more clearly. And so on.

This doesn't mean you can't have a grand vision—there's no reason you can't have a map for the journey. But a map won't show you the potholes or the weather. For that, you just have to take it step-by-step.

Every person who ever left what they hated to find what they loved started with one step. They made a move—just one. Every journey really does begin with a single step. There are absolutely no exceptions to this rule.

The part they don't tell you is that the size of the step matters.

Any time you find yourself stuck or procrastinating, dig deeper, and you'll find that the first step is either too large or too vague. When that happens, get micro. Think tiny and think clear. Find the smallest possible step that has no ambiguity and carries as little fear as possible.

Quitting isn't a giant leap. It's not a moon landing. Quitting is a *step*. Preferably the tiniest one possible from the cliff's edge onto the first trapeze bar.

Then you repeat. You can make the whole journey that way—looking only as far as your headlights allow.

QUITTERS LIKE YOU

JAKE "EJ" CELLER
Chief Visionary Officer and Cofounder, Secure-Centric

My dad wanted to be an entrepreneur his whole life. He was a successful businessman and eventually became the COO of a big textile company. While he worked there for more than ten years, he hated every day of it.

He had always wanted to start his own business but never made the leap, mainly because he was making a lot of money and had kids. At age forty-seven, he finally started his own business. When it failed after three years, my father ended up retiring and raising me. He told me that his one regret in life was he didn't start his business sooner.

That stuck with me my whole childhood. But when I got out of school, it wasn't long before I found myself in a similar trap. At age twenty-six, I was an enterprise account rep, and I was making great money. I enjoyed my job, but I yearned to do more with my life than sell technology to businesses. Like my dad, I stayed because of the income. It was the classic "golden handcuffs" situation.

Last February, my dad passed away. This gave me a massive push to do something more with my life. I realized that to take the next step, I would have to surround myself with business owners, so I started talking with as many owners as I could and joined a mastermind group. I also started a few side hustles, including a small tech business as well as renovating and flipping real estate.

The side hustles during my W-2 time were really important. They gave me some extra cash flow, but they also helped me decide what was worth pursuing. Ultimately, I listed my side hustles on a whiteboard and asked myself which had the greatest revenue potential. I realized that the tech business had exponentially more upside than flipping real estate and my W-2 combined.

After having some thirty conversations with people who had left their W-2s and getting support from my mom, I finally made the commitment to leave.

I created a robust W-2 escape plan that included getting very clear about my burn rate and what I'd need in the bank. This helped me know how much time I had before my business would have to pay me a salary.

I can't explain to you the beauty of living a life as a business owner. There is so much power in becoming an orchestrator. I can focus on only the most essential tasks and delegate the rest. While I have not found my purpose yet, my curiosity and passion fuel me every day and generate exponential personal growth. I can't wait to continue this awesome ride!

THE LESSONS

A side hustle can be a powerful tool.

Surrounding yourself with other Quitters
can be life-changing.

A clear financial plan includes
a safety net and road map.

DIP YOUR TOES IN

Back when Pat was a college student, he got a summer job at a deli near the beach. The job was cutting meat, and it paid three bucks an hour. It wasn't glamorous, but it was a job.

Pat's friend, meanwhile, had stumbled on a new gig selling timeshare appointments. He'd hang out on the boardwalk, offering tourists a chance to visit a resort in return for a $50 steakhouse gift certificate. For each successful appointment, Pat's buddy got $20.

Twenty dollars for a single sale sounded a lot better than cutting meat all day to make the same money. Pat decided to give it a shot on his day off.

On day one, Pat showed up as instructed and followed the instructions: Wear a collared shirt, ditch the sunglasses, and be personable. A few minutes later, he was off and running.

The timeshare company had a daily sales scoreboard. Each salesperson had a number; Pat was #101. In the morning, all the sales and commissions were posted for everyone to see.

The golden boy of boardwalk sales was #33, Danny. He always took the top slot, leading the board. A typical day might see a listing at the top like, *#33—2x$20* or *#33—4x$20*.

Pat had no idea how his first day had gone, but on day two, he showed up for the morning meeting to pick up his pay—if there was any. He joined the rest of the team to watch as the numbers went up on the board.

The first line read, *#101—5x$20*. Pat had nailed the top spot.

Not two seconds later, a loud voice came from the back of the room. It was Danny.

"Who the fuck is 101?" he hollered.

There was a new golden boy in boardwalk sales.

THE LOW-RISK TRY

Pat never went back to the deli. He could make almost as much in a day as he did in a week slicing meat. In fact, that gig was Pat's first commission-only job, and he never looked back.

The real lesson here isn't the cash. It's that Pat tested the waters *before* quitting. He had no idea if he'd be good at it or whether he'd like it. To find out, he simply went down to the beach and dipped his toes in the water, so to speak. His biggest risk was losing a sunny day off trying something new.

In the business world, there's a similar strategy called the "minimum viable product" (MVP).

It asks the question: What is the simplest working version of a product that we can get customers using?

In tech startups, it often means making a functional version of an app that people can use. It's something a company can make as quickly and inexpensively as possible, so prospective customers can try it and provide feedback.

The idea is that the MVP lets you learn quickly and inexpensively so you can ultimately create something far better than you could by spending a zillion dollars over many years working in a vacuum.

Like Pat's boardwalk sales experiment, the focus of the MVP is on learning. Rather than guessing at what customers want, what might work, or how best to create something, you start with a simple experiment. You dip your toes in and test the waters.

Dipping your toes is all about the trapeze. Rather than trying to leap across the chasm to the end goal, you do a short swing and hope to learn something that helps guide your next swing. And so on. For example:

- You want to offer a service. What if you just build a one-page website and see if someone says yes?
- You want to buy a rental property. What if you rent out a room in your house and see what you think?
- You want to try a new profession. Can you spend a day with someone who already does it?

Trials and experiments. Pop-up stores. Side hustles. Temporary contracts. Prototypes. Job shadowing. Coffee dates. Market surveys. Like the MVP approach, these tiny swings are focused on learning.

What is the simplest way to test-drive your plan?

RANK YOUR SIDE HUSTLE

List any current or future side hustles, experiments, trials, or other ways that you can dip your toes in and test your plan. For each, list the time required and the potential income.

There's no objective right answer, just a right answer for you. For example, if your current job is demanding, then you might want to test ideas that don't take long. If money is critical, then you might want the side hustle that can put money in your account the fastest.

SIDE HUSTLE	TIME REQUIRED	$ PAYOUT

TOOL #15

FOCUS ON THE PROCESS

They say that Michelangelo used to see his sculptures in his mind as if they were already complete. All he had to do to create *David*, for example, was take a big block of marble and just chip away all the bits that weren't *David*. Voilà: masterpiece.

What an amazing concept. Too bad it's complete nonsense. As far as anyone knows, he never actually said or did anything of the sort. Michelangelo *toiled*, like all of us. He had doubts. He changed his mind partway through projects. He left lots of work unfinished.

Does that sound like a guy who's just casually chipping away all the parts that aren't the masterpiece? Quite the opposite. You can bet Mike had plenty of lousy days working on *David*. There were days he wasn't sure how it was going to turn out—or if it would turn out at all.

In other words, Michelangelo was a human facing the cliff, just like you. Each trapeze swing was a little leap into the unknown.

In the end, though, Michelangelo swung the hammer at the chisel enough times to produce something that mattered. He showed up; he did the work. He followed a process that involved moving gradually closer to where he wanted to be.

Was it easy? No. Was it messy? Sure. But it got him there.

JUST DO TODAY

The future is not yours to know. All you can do is show up, do the work, and trust the process to get you a little closer to your goal all the time.

There is no process-free path. Michelangelo didn't swing the hammer once and get *David*. You don't get to swing on one trapeze bar and arrive. There's no leaping straight to the end state, going from the job you hate to the work you love in one brief moment of courage. It doesn't work that way. Like Michelangelo hammering away at the stone, you don't just create your final work with one blow. You have to keep coming back.

What is your process? What's the work to be done on the day, in the moment?

Bonus fact: Michelangelo created *David* from a discarded block of marble. Yep—it was a chunk of rock that other artists had decided was unworkable.

You don't need a perfect vision, and you can't always see the future. What you can do is focus on the process that gets you closer to what you want each day.

QUITTERS LIKE YOU

CAROLE JENSEN
Mobile Notary Public

I worked an eight-to-five job in the title-and-escrow industry for more than thirty-five years. I could never understand how someone could work a commission job not knowing what money would be coming in on a regular basis. Survival is instinctual in all of us, and my survival was tied to my job. My paycheck, health care, and 401(k) were my security.

I worked in different roles at many title companies and enjoyed each position because I was learning new things. But it wasn't all glorious. At times, I felt misunderstood and had a feeling that there was something missing, something else out there. As time went on, that feeling grew stronger. I longed for adventure, new places, and new people, but I continued on the same journey thinking that if I changed course, then my security would be gone … and then what?

It took many years for me to become brave. I tested the waters every now and then by traveling, exploring, and connecting with people who were on their own paths, but I still didn't venture off my secure paved road. The fear of cutting myself off from my tried-and-true profession was too great.

One year, I watched a friend kayak from Monterey, California, to Waikiki, Hawaii, in the Great Pacific Race. It took the crew of two men and two women over a month to finish. It was quite something to watch, but at that moment I realized I was tired of being a spectator. I was determined to have my own adventure. Not long after, I watched *The Way* with Martin Sheen and Emilio Estevez, about walking the Camino de Santiago, an ancient pilgrimage trail in Spain. Instantly, I said to myself, "This is my adventure!"

I spent the next year training and researching for my trip, and I made it happen. It was the best decision of my life, so far. That was the turning point—I went back to the same job, but something had changed in me. I was no longer waiting and watching; I had become an active participant.

During the pandemic, the need for mobile notaries skyrocketed. I was a certified notary public for my job, so there was a natural fit for me to make the transition to entrepreneur. I marketed myself to people at my previous title-company employers, and I was on my way.

It has only been a few months since I've "retired," but in that time, I have created my own business, connected with people who I am sure will now be my mentors, made new friends, started swimming again, read books I've been meaning to finish, and rented an Airbnb in San Diego for a month. My time in San Diego gave me space to reflect and adjust. Leaving something you have done for so long is a big shock, so this helped with the transition. I highly recommend quitting one thing to add something else you enjoy to your life. I am grateful to have the flexibility to work when I want and as much as I want, while balancing the things I want to do at this stage of my life.

I am not sure where I will end up, but I am open to the possibilities. It feels like a new beginning. I count my blessings daily!

If you find yourself at a crossroads, I think Dr. Seuss said it best:

> You have brains in your head.
> You have feet in your shoes.
> You can steer yourself
> any direction you choose.

LESSONS

It's never too late to start something new.

Sometimes, the courage to quit comes from being courageous elsewhere in your life.

Quitting can be a shock. Make sure you have a meaningful way to fill your time.

BE AGGRESSIVELY PATIENT

When Tim created his first Quit Plan, the end goal was to move to the mountains. That plan had a five-year horizon.

It didn't quite work out that way. Three years later, Tim was celebrating his fortieth birthday, but his vision for the future didn't seem to be materializing.

What did he do? He went back to his plan and updated it. He examined what was working and what wasn't. He changed what needed to be changed. Then he chose to be what we call "aggressively patient."

It's a funny term. An oxymoron, really. How can you be aggressive *and* patient? What it really means is to view the act of patience as a form of action—as something you do.

Being patient is not the same as simply waiting. Waiting is doing nothing and hoping that what you want will arrive. Waiting for a better work-life situation than the one you have is just wishing, nothing more.

Patience is doing the work now, knowing that the results from that work can take time to arrive, like planting seeds for a future harvest.

Aggressive patience is about understanding that action and results are not the same thing. You plant seeds, but you don't grow the plants. Your actions may create results, but they *aren't* the results. Those come later.

Not only must you be patient with your new business or career, but you must also be patient with your evolving self. Remember that each move, each trapeze swing, is a shift in identity. You're gradually recreating yourself, and that won't happen overnight.

Aggressive patience also lies at the intersection of gas and brake. It's about using both judiciously. Too much gas and you can swing your trapeze wildly out of control. Too much brake and you fall into ready, aim, ready, aim, ready, aim—but you never fire.

Tim's aggressive patience was eventually rewarded. He kept moving forward while detaching from the timeline as necessary.

Likewise, if you keep working, adjusting, and working the process again, you'll get somewhere. The results will come. You will, as Tim says, "get the goods in the woods."

Note: Tim's personal planning documents for his transition are remarkable reading. You can find them at www.bigger pockets.com/quitters.

USE CONSTRAINTS TO COMMIT

Brooks's law states that adding more resources to a software project that's running late makes it even later. Software engineer Fred Brooks's famous analogy was that a woman can make a baby in nine months, but nine women can't make a baby in one month. In other words, adding more isn't always helpful. More women won't speed up baby-making. More money doesn't always get the software done faster. More time or research won't make you quit sooner.

What do you do if more won't help? Try the opposite: less. Less is about constraints. It's about setting boundaries on time, resources, and choices, and you can use it to your advantage.

HOW TO COMMIT TO YOUR QUIT

Commitments are a form of constraint. When you tell your friend you'll meet them at the gym at 7:00 a.m., you're making a social commitment that increases your odds of following through. When you hire a personal trainer to meet you at the gym at 7:00 a.m., you're making a financial commitment because you're paying for that time, whether you go or not. And when you pay that trainer to show up at your house at

7:00 a.m.? That's a logistic commitment because you're then forced by circumstance to do that workout.

You can use these same levers to take the first step in your quit (or any step after). For example:

- Signing a lease is a commitment to your new business.
- Telling three friends your quit date is a commitment to moving forward.
- Hiring a business coach is a commitment to education and accountability.
- Listing a room for rent in your home, reading Bigger-Pockets books, and listening to the *BiggerPockets Podcast* are all commitments to a tiny step in your brand-new real estate side hustle.

At the extreme end of the commitment scale, you can also burn ships. If you quit your job, for example, you'll have no choice but to move forward in some way. Burning your bridges, of course, is leaping. It's risky. But there are times when the only way to grab onto that first trapeze bar is to burn the platform you're standing on.

If you're having trouble committing, stop looking for more. Perhaps you don't need more time, more money, or more options. Maybe less is the secret to moving forward.

QUITTERS LIKE YOU

JOSEPH WECHSLER
Managing Director and Founder, Blueline Ventures

I spent the first two years out of college in real estate development and construction management. After that, I started my own company with a partner, but I had always dreamed of being in management consulting, so I went back to grad school full-time, got my MBA, and soon landed at the large consulting firm PricewaterhouseCoopers.

I was happy there. I was doing really well and was on a partner track. My wife and I also started having children. I was on the road full-time and so we moved to Charleston, where we had a supportive network of family and friends. But I was always away, sometimes three weeks at a time. I was in some forty countries during those five or six years. The time away left me homesick, and it pained me to feel like my kids were growing up without me.

I started reaching out to local companies and linked up with a guy who had a small consulting firm in Charleston. I took a pay cut to join him, with the end goal of growing the company and gaining equity in it. Things went well, and eighteen months ago, we sold our company to a larger consulting firm.

The integration with the company we sold to wasn't going well, however. As part of the agreement, I stayed on as an employee, but the dynamics of the new owners' personalities were hard to deal with. With someone else running the show, it felt like my input didn't matter anymore. At the same time, I was learning a lot more about financial independence and what was important for me and my family. I began speaking to people who had achieved financial freedom and started reading books like *Buy Then Build*.

I decided last November that I had to find a way out. I knew deep down that I was thinking about life and my career in the right way for the first time. I had a pretty good financial runway, and I knew our family could change spending habits if necessary. In the worst-case scenario, if I reached the end of that runway and nothing significant materialized, I could get another job.

I wanted to work for myself, so I set out looking for a company I could buy instead of starting one from scratch. My criteria were that the company have a manager or team in place that would make the transition with me—I didn't want to buy myself a harder job—and that it was a business where I wasn't the one delivering the revenue. With consulting, 100 percent of my income had been tied to the hours I had put in.

To make a long story short, my last day (and last paycheck)

was June 30, 2021. I'm now buying three companies from two sellers, all in the senior-care space. Both sellers are absentee owners, so I'm confident there is opportunity for growth and that the companies can run without my being a daily part of them.

When I decided to quit, the thing that I was most nervous about was leaving a company where I felt like I was a critical component. I know everybody's replaceable, and I'm definitely no exception, but I was worried about what would happen to this small company and its team in my absence. I spoke to a psychologist/career coach who helped me understand that those things were not my problem or within my control.

I realized that I was happy working from home, having flexibility, and being super productive. In every other job I've had, I've been expected to be there fifty hours per week, and in reality, there's not usually fifty hours of work to do. Now I'm able to accomplish a lot in just a couple of hours every day. I've kept one project with the old company as an independent contractor. It's my side hustle—fewer than ten hours per week. I'm not burning bridges, and I maintain a relationship with my partner.

THE LESSONS

You don't need to quit alone.

Don't burn bridges unnecessarily.

Buying a business can be easier than starting one.

TOOL #18
STOP NOT QUITTING

Author Anne Lamott wrote a best-selling book on writing called *Bird by Bird*. It's sold a zillion copies. Aspiring authors around the world adore the book, especially the advice that inspired the title, which is to take things step-by-step.

When asked why she thought the book was so successful, Lamott says in part that it's because she doesn't try to teach people how to write—she teaches them how to stop *not* writing.

That's advice that any Quitter can use.

You can't quit your job *and* keep working at it. But if you've been feeling stuck, there's a good chance that's exactly what you have been doing. You're trying to have it both ways. You're swinging out—maybe dabbling here, investigating there. You're making big plans. You're mapping out a vision. You're doing your research. But with each one of those little swings out from the cliff edge, you just hang onto the bar and swing back in again.

Can you overlap? Sure. Can you do work and have a side hustle? Sure. But if you hate your job, doing it half the time is like taking half a dose of poison and expecting to feel great. You're still headed for trouble; you're just taking your time getting there.

You want to quit? Then stop not quitting. Everything you do each day that isn't quitting is a vote for things to stay the same. Every day that repeats like the previous is a commitment to not changing.

Can you change safely? Yes. Can you take baby steps? Sure. Can you build a safety net? Of course. But one day, you're going to have done everything you can except for the thing that makes all the difference: quit.

SWING!

KEY INSIGHTS

TOOL #12

FAILURE-PROOF YOUR MIND DAILY
Each day, do what puts you in
the best mental, emotional, and physical place
to perform your best.

TOOL #13

FIND THE SMALLEST POSSIBLE STEP
What's the smallest action you can take
to move forward?

TOOL #14

DIP YOUR TOES IN
How can you test-drive your vision?

TOOL #15

FOCUS ON THE PROCESS
You can only do today's work.

TOOL #16

BE AGGRESSIVELY PATIENT
Your job is to take the action, not to create results.

TOOL #17

USE CONSTRAINTS TO COMMIT
How can less, not more, help you make progress?

TOOL #18

STOP NOT QUITTING
Every day you don't do something different is a
commitment to not changing.

THE END

A FINAL NOTE FROM TIM AND PAT

The caterpillar turning into the beautiful butterfly is an age-old metaphor for transformation. You start out sluggish and slow but become graceful, beautiful, and inspiring. It's everyone's favorite kind of transformation—a sort of magic trick where you step through a door and come out the other side and everything is amazing.

It turns out the caterpillar's real transformation is quite different from the one depicted in stories. The caterpillar creates the cocoon, yes, but it doesn't go on to grow gossamer wings and burst from the shell like a supermodel onto a catwalk. What really happens is that the caterpillar releases enzymes that dissolve it into a kind of caterpillar soup. Then the butterfly is built from scratch using stem cells. Insert sad trombone sound.

At first, this explanation feels a little disappointing. Like finding out something beautiful turned out to be fake. But there's a lot to be learned from the true story of the caterpillar. First, note that the caterpillar creates its own cocoon. Your current reality is no different. You chose your current job. You said yes. You may have felt like you didn't have better options, but you still built the cocoon you're in. If you've said yes to what you have now, you can also say yes to something new.

Notice that when the butterfly leaves the cocoon, it feels a bit like an escape—an elaborate prison break that ends with a new and improved life. Quitting is undoubtedly a kind of escape too. You leave the "prison" of that horrible job, those loathsome meetings, or the pointless reports, and you take your first sweet breath of freedom. (Ideally, your gorgeous soulmate also picks you up in a Lamborghini outside, but let's not take the prison-movie analogy too far.)

The part that's most overlooked, however, is the whole dissolving thing. That is a requirement. For you to find and say yes to the thing you really want requires to some extent that you become a different person. Like the caterpillar and the butterfly, you can't be two complete things at once. You don't need to change your personality or your body or your friends or your values, but you will need to shift your identity. You'll have to dissolve a little of the old you—the one who is thinking the old thoughts and doing the old things.

If you've always been an employee, for example, then that is wrapped up in your identity. You might even hear it in your language:

- "I'm not business-minded."
- "I have to have a secure job."
- "I'm not a risk-taker."

Those are all identity statements. The tricky thing about identity statements is that they tend to become true if we keep saying them. You are, after all, creating your future right now by the things you think, say, and do.

What if you begin to shift those statements to serve Future You—that magnificent butterfly that's being created from Past You?

- "I haven't learned a lot about business yet."
- "I like to feel secure, so I'm being very deliberate."
- "I'm a calculated risk-taker."

These new statements don't deny the old you. They acknowledge the existence of the caterpillar. But each one dissolves the old caterpillar a little and begins the process of creating the butterfly from the same essence.

EVERYBODY LOVES A QUITTER

We began this journey by exploring the idea that "nobody loves a Quitter." Sometimes that's true. Nobody loves someone who gives up just because things get a little uncomfortable. Nobody loves someone unreliable. Nobody loves someone they can't count on.

But there are Quitters who people love. Your kids love it when they can see that the world really is full of possibility and that dreaming big is more than okay—it's a stepping stone to something better. Your spouse loves it when you're fulfilled and have a sense of purpose that not only gets you out of bed but also brings you home filled with contagious energy.

Your colleagues at the job you're leaving? Believe it or not, they love it when you leave. Really, they do; you weren't your best self there anyway. For the aspiring Quitters at your old job, you're also a tiny beacon of possibility that might just light them up when they need it the most.

Your new colleagues and partners? They love how alive you are and how much passion you bring to the work.

And your friends? Wow. They love how much better you can support them when you're fulfilled yourself.

It turns out almost *everyone* loves a Quitter. Because everybody loves it when you don't give up on yourself.

IT'S NOT ABOUT THE JOB

That's the message we heard time and time again from Quitters: "It's not about the job." Whether they were leaving a W-2 that paid well or an entry-level job that didn't even pay the bills; whether they were jumping ship from a Fortune 500 or ditching a decades-long career, the sentiment was the same. It wasn't about the old thing.

It didn't seem to matter what Quitters were headed toward either. It might be a small business. Maybe a side hustle. Maybe a big business. It could be a different job in the same field. It might even be a different job at the same company or a return to school. In the end, for all of them, it wasn't about the old job or the new one. It was about how the world feels when you are taking control.

Freedom. Possibility. Confidence. Hope. That's what quitting is really about. It's about feeling like tomorrow matters.

Like you're setting a good example for your loved ones. Like you're making your own decisions (and your own mistakes). So, no, it's not about the job. It's about being the boss—of your life.

If you take away one thing from the book, make it that. Quitting is about taking charge. About deciding that this is *your* life, and no matter what happens, it'll be a better one if you feel like you get to choose.

Choose whatever you want. Choose what gets you out of bed in the morning. Choose whatever turns your crank, eases your pain, or floats your boat.

But *choose*. Because that's where the magic is.

Get after it,

Tim and Pat

THE QUITTER'S CHECKLIST

- [ ] Acknowledge the Truth
- [ ] Understand Risk and Reward
- [ ] Ask the Failure Questions
- [ ] Accept the Realistic Worst-Case Scenario
- [ ] Follow the Fear
- [ ] Check the Suck Meter
- [ ] Weave Your Financial Net
- [ ] Decide What Success Looks Like
- [ ] Build Your Plan B
- [ ] Gather a Quit Team
- [ ] Plan For Obstacles
- [ ] Failure-Proof Your Mind Daily
- [ ] Find the Smallest Possible Step
- [ ] Dip Your Toes In
- [ ] Focus On the Process
- [ ] Be Aggressively Patient
- [ ] Use Constraints to Commit
- [ ] Stop Not Quitting

ACKNOWLEDGMENTS

We will keep our acknowledgments short and sweet.

First, we acknowledge our partners in the Quitter's Club, Aaron Velky and Ian Lobas. Our efforts to change the world by helping millions live lives of passion are only coming true through your efforts. We are so grateful that you get us and get the movement.

Next, we want to acknowledge Dan Clements: author, writer, collaborator. Without you, this project would have never come together as fast and professionally as it has. Thank you also to our BiggerPockets publishing, editorial, design, and marketing teams that worked on this book.

We want to acknowledge Nick Johnson. When we decided to write this book, you had already done over a year of research into this exact subject, and you have been so generous in sharing everything you learned in incredible detail.

Last, to all the Quitters out there taking the risks daily to make their careers and lives better. We wrote this book for you to not feel so alone. Take the leap for life!

You're not alone.

Download our FREE playbook,
join the mastermind, get coaching, and
hang around other Quitters like you.

Go to
**www.biggerpockets.com/
quitters**
for more.

More from
BiggerPockets Publishing

If you enjoyed this book, we hope you'll take a moment to check out some of the other great material BiggerPockets offers. Whether you crave freedom or stability, a back-up plan, or passive income, BiggerPockets empowers you to live life on your own terms through real estate investing. Find the information, inspiration, and tools you need to dive right into the world of real estate investing with confidence.

Sign up today—**IT'S FREE!**
Visit www.BiggerPockets.com

Find our books at
www.BiggerPockets.com/store

First-Time Home Buyer: The Complete Playbook to Avoiding Rookie Mistakes

Everything you need to buy your first home, from initial decisions all the way to the closing table! Scott Trench and Mindy Jensen of the BiggerPockets Money Podcast have been buying and selling houses for a collective thirty years. In this book, they'll give you a comprehensive overview of the home-buying process so you can consider all of your options and avoid pitfalls while jumping into the big, bad role of homeowner.

More from
BiggerPockets Publishing

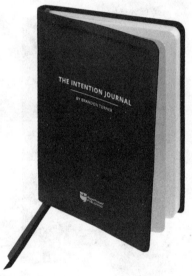

The Intention Journal
Some people can achieve great wealth, rock-solid relationships, age-defying health, and remarkable happiness—and so many others struggle, fail, and give up on their dreams, goals, and ambitions. Could it simply be that those who find success are more intentional about it? Once you build intentionality into your daily routine, you can achieve the incredible success that sometimes seems out of reach. Backed by the latest research in psychology, this daily planner offers an effective framework to set, review, and accomplish your goals.

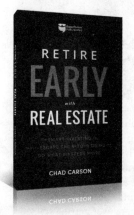

More from
BiggerPockets Publishing

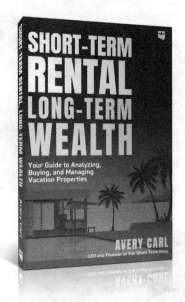

Short-Term Rental, Long-Term Wealth: Your Guide to Analyzing, Buying, and Managing Vacation Properties
From analyzing potential properties to effectively managing your listings, this book is your one-stop resource for making a profit with short-term rentals! Airbnb, Vrbo, and other listing services have become massively popular in recent years—why not tap into the gold mine? Avery Carl will show you how to choose, acquire, and manage a short-term rental from anywhere in the country, plus how to avoid common pitfalls and overcome obstacles that keep many would-be investors from ever getting started.

CONNECT WITH BIGGERPOCKETS

and Become Successful in Your Real Estate Business Today!

Facebook
/BiggerPockets

Instagram
@BiggerPockets

Twitter
@BiggerPockets

LinkedIn
/company/Bigger
Pockets

Website
BiggerPockets.com